Savvy

ME Time

HOW TO MANAGE A BUSY LIFE

AUBRE ANDRUS

with Karen Bluth, PhD

illustrations by Veronica Collignon

CAPSTONE PRESS
a capstone imprint

Savvy Books are published by Capstone Press
1710 Roe Crest Drive, North Mankato, Minnesota 56003
www.mycapstone.com

Library of Congress Cataloging-in-Publication Data

Names: Andrus, Aubre, author. | Bluth, Karen.
Title: Me time : how to manage a busy life / by Aubre Andrus, Karen Bluth,
PhD, University of North Carolina, Chapel Hill, NC.
Description: North Mankato, MN : Capstone Press, [2017] | Series:
Stress-busting survival guides | Audience: Grade 7 to 8.
Identifiers: LCCN 2017005174 | ISBN 9781515768210 (library binding)
Subjects: LCSH: Time management—Juvenile literature. | Self—Juvenile
literature. | Self-actualization (Psychology)—Juvenile literature.
Classification: LCC HD69.T54 A53 2017 | DDC 650.1/1—dc23
LC record available at https://lccn.loc.gov/2017005174

Editor: Eliza Leahy
Designer: Tracy McCabe
Art Director: Kay Fraser
Production Specialist: Tori Abraham

Illustrations by Veronica Collignon;
Photographs by Capstone Studio: TJ Thoraldson Digital Photography, 17 (both), 18, 19; Shutterstock:
Aleshyn_Andrei, 44, everst, 24, groodday28, 13 (left), iordani, 38, Jacob Lund, 26, 28, 29, Jaren Jai
Wicklund, 42, Olga Danylenko, 14, PHOTOCREO Michal Bednarek, 13 (right), Rawpixel.com, 12, Shining
stars, 35, T.Dallas, 8, Tiplyashina Evgeniya, 34, val lawless, 15, Who is Danny, 10, yougoigo, 36
Design Elements by Capstone and Shutterstock
author photo by Ariel Andrus, 48 (top)

Consultant and contributing author: Karen Bluth, PhD
University of North Carolina, Chapel Hill
Chapel Hill, NC

Printed and bound in the United States of America.
010373F17

Table of Contents

How to Use This Book

Organized! Confident! Relaxed! Wouldn't you love to feel that way right now? With this book, you can. Really. Because even when you're feeling the exact opposite — overwhelmed, stressed out, and way too busy — there are tips and tricks that can totally transform your mindset and your emotions. This book will fill you in.

Flip through the following pages and choose the idea that piques your interest. There's no wrong or right answer, and no true beginning or end. The most important thing is that you stop for a second and take some time to focus on yourself.

Prioritize "me" time — and don't feel guilty about it. All you have to do is turn the page. You've got this!

However, you can't use this book to solve serious mental health problems such as anxiety disorders, depression, or eating disorders. If at any point you think you need more help than this book can offer, please turn to page 44.

IF YOU FEEL LIKE YOU NEVER HAVE ENOUGH TIME → LEARN HOW TO SPEND IT MORE WISELY ON PAGE 10.

IF YOU FEEL COMPLETELY OVERWHELMED → LEARN HOW VISUALIZATION CAN CALM YOU DOWN ON PAGE 12.

IF YOU CAN'T FIND ANYTHING → TRY THE ROOM ORGANIZATION TIPS ON PAGE 20.

IF YOU CAN'T STAY FOCUSED → FLIP TO PAGE 38 FOR SOME PRODUCTIVITY TRICKS.

IF STRESS IS KEEPING YOU FROM A GOOD NIGHT'S SLEEP → TRY THE TIPS ON PAGE 41.

Just Breathe

Begin this exercise by stepping into a quiet area and trying to relax. When you focus on your breathing, you will simply watch and feel your breath. Deep breathing sends signals to the body to calm down. It can make the mind clearer, and it delivers more oxygen to the lungs and heart.

Sit cross-legged or lie on a yoga mat — whatever is most comfortable! The following breathing exercises are organized by difficulty, from easier to more challenging.

ABDOMINAL BREATHING

When to do it: Before a stressful event or when you're feeling nervous
How to do it: Place one hand on your chest and the other on your belly. Inhale deeply, then exhale deeply. Notice the slight change in sensations as your chest rises and then falls. Repeat as many times as you'd like.
What it does: This breathing method helps you find focus and peace.

EQUAL BREATHING

When to do it: When you're trying to meditate
How to do it: Inhale deeply for four seconds, then exhale deeply for four seconds. Repeat as many times as you'd like.
What it does: This is a relaxing exercise.

ALTERNATE NOSTRIL BREATHING

When to do it: When you need to focus
How to do it: Cover your left nostril and breathe in, then move your finger to cover your right nostril and breathe out. Now breathe in through your left nostril, then move your finger to cover your left nostril and breathe out. Repeat as many times as you'd like.
What it does: This exercise is energizing.

RELAXING BREATH

When to do it: When you need to fall asleep
How to do it: Inhale for four seconds, then exhale for eight seconds. Repeat five times.
What it does: This exercise is a natural tranquilizer.

STIMULATING BREATH

When to do it: When you need a confidence boost
How to do it: Inhale and exhale rapidly through your nose while keeping your mouth lightly closed. Do this for no more than ten seconds.
What it does: This invigorating exercise gives you an energy boost and focus.

"I'D RATHER REGRET THE THINGS I'VE DONE THAN REGRET THE THINGS I HAVEN'T DONE." - LUCILLE BALL

Manage Your Time

Fitting school, fun, family, friends, and sports or other activities into one day can seem impossible. But with a plan, each day will become much more manageable, and you may even feel more productive. These time management tips can keep you motivated, on schedule, and could create some room in your schedule for a relaxing break!

PRIORITIZE

To-do lists are great, but when they're 15 items long, it's very unlikely you'll get to everything by the end of the day. Instead of making the world's longest to-do list, choose the three most important things that have to be completed each day, and make sure you accomplish those tasks.

BREAK IT DOWN

If you have an overwhelming project due next month or a big goal you'd like to reach, break it into chunks. How can a project or goal be separated into smaller milestones? Set deadlines for each portion of your project or goal and write down the timeline into your planner or your calendar. For example, if you have a presentation due in history class in three weeks, break it into three portions. Week one: gather notes and draft an outline of your presentation. Week two: begin working on your slideshow or poster and picking out the most important information to include. Week three: practice your oral presentation and make your visual presentation look clean and professional.

SET BOUNDARIES

One of the reasons why it's hard to be productive is because we are constantly trying to multitask. If you need to spend an hour doing homework, do it fully and without apology. Shut off your phone and computer, close your bedroom door, and don't let anything break your focus. If you are prioritizing family time this week and need to miss a friend's party for your grandpa's birthday, be upfront. You can make time for your= friends another weekend.

REMOVE WHAT YOU CAN

It's easy to overcommit. Ask yourself what can wait? What can you say no to? Maybe your laundry can wait until Saturday or that movie you promised your sister you'd go to can wait until next weekend. Finding balance is important, but so is being realistic with what you need to do and how you're going to do it.

FOCUS ON THE BIG PICTURE

If you're a perfectionist, you may be wasting precious time obsessing over the details. Sometimes "good enough" is great! Don't be so hard on yourself. Give yourself permission to *not* go above and beyond every time.

"ALWAYS TRY TO GET BETTER. EVERY TIME YOU DO SOMETHING. YOU DON'T HAVE TO GET IT PERFECT EVERY TIME." – JENNIE CHEN

Create a Time Budget

You're at the mall with friends and you have $40. You buy a shirt for $30 and lunch for $10. Now your friends want to get ice cream, but you can't because you've already spent your budget.

Imagine if you treated time the same way you treat money. There are 24 hours in each day. So how will you best spend each one? Creating a time budget is a daily practice that can help you manage stress, be more productive, and make sure there's still time for fun.

24-HOUR BUDGET

TAKE OUT A PIECE OF BLANK PAPER. DRAW FOUR COLUMNS ON YOUR PAGE, TITLED "SPEND," "SAVE," "INVEST," AND "GIVE." FOLLOW THE STEPS BELOW TO COME UP WITH A 24-HOUR TIME BUDGET TAILORED JUST FOR YOU.

1. SPEND

Write down the amount of hours you spend in a day on "non-negotiable" commitments such as school, sleep, and getting ready each morning. Tally up the total.

2. SAVE

List some of your favorite ways to spend "me time" and how long each idea takes. For example, reading a novel for one hour, going for a 30-minute run, or winding down before bed (see page 42).

3. INVEST

Tally up how long you need each day to reach your goals and accomplish tasks. Taking a drawing class for one hour or spending two hours on homework are great examples.

4. GIVE

Consider how much time you'd like to spend each day on others. It could be volunteering, spending quality time with your family, or hanging out with your friends.

5. COMPLETE YOUR SCHEDULE

Now comes the challenging part — trying to fit all your ideas into 24 hours. On a new sheet of paper, create an hour-by-hour schedule for one day. Once you've completed it, you'll become more aware of how you are spending your time. When you have a good idea of how you're spending 24 hours, try creating a weeklong time budget.

Visualize

Visualization is the practice of creating a mental image. The technique is often used to help professionals such as athletes, actors, doctors, and lawyers prepare for big events. You can use visualization as a rehearsal for a challenge you're about to take on, or you can use it as an escape when you're feeling stressed. It can give you more confidence or give you a sense of calm — either way, it's good for you!

When you practice visualization, it's important to consider all five senses. What are you smelling? Hearing? Feeling? Seeing? Tasting? Try visualizing for five minutes each night before bed.

Before you start visualizing, find a quiet place to sit or lie down, then close your eyes.

IF YOU'RE THINKING, "I NEED TO STEP AWAY FOR A MINUTE."

Think of this visualization as a break that will help you relax when you're feeling particularly overwhelmed.

Brush any stressful or concerning images to the side and make room for some good thoughts.

Close your eyes. Imagine your body is so light that it floats off the ground and soars gracefully into the sky. Picture what your home or school looks like from above. Now imagine yourself soaring through the clouds. Look below. What do you see? Now look above and admire the never-ending sky. When you're ready, gently float back down to Earth. Land softly in the grass in your front yard or in your favorite park. Take a few more deep breaths. When you're ready, open your eyes.

IF YOU'RE THINKING, "I NEED TO GET OUT OF HERE."

When you're feeling stressed out, a mental vacation is almost as good as a real one.

Imagine a secluded beach or another serene place, such as a cabin in a quiet forest; a kayak on a smooth, clear lake; or a bench in a sunny park. Now imagine you're in that perfect place, seeing it through your own eyes. Think about your other senses and the ways the environment is calming each one.

Visualization exercises can also help you fall asleep.

IF YOU'RE THINKING, "I CAN DO THIS . . .
BUT I'M NERVOUS."

This visualization can bring you courage when you need it most.

Find a comfortable position on the ground with your legs crossed or kneeling, then close your eyes and straighten your back and shoulders. Breathe deeply in and out. When your breath is steady, begin to imagine a majestic mountain in front of you. Admire it from afar. Visualize the trees, sky, and water surrounding it. Then "zoom in" your focus to the mountain. Get closer, and closer. Now imagine you are the mountain — its peak is your head and its base is your legs. No matter what the season, the mountain sits unchanged and strong. Visualize the mountain standing strong through changes in foliage, snowfall, rainstorms, intense heat, and dense fog. No matter what comes your way, you can sit unchanged and strong, like the mountain. When you're ready, open your eyes.

IF YOU'RE THINKING, "I COULD NEVER DO THAT."

Through your own eyes, imagine yourself doing the action you believe you cannot do. Visualize every single step of the way. For instance, if you want to learn how to play a song on the guitar, imagine yourself opening your guitar case, picking up the guitar, touching each string, reading the music notes, strumming each chord, and hearing the song come together. You could even imagine yourself messing up a note, then recovering quickly. Sometimes it can be helpful to realize that making a mistake doesn't mean failure.

IF YOU'RE THINKING, "I CAN'T BELIEVE THAT HAPPENED."

It's usually not helpful to dwell on the past, but if something is bothering you and you just can't shake it, visualization can help. Imagine the moment as a movie, but change anything about the scene for the better. Fix your mistakes, change what you said, or alter what someone else did. Replay the revised version in your head a few times. Then move on.

IF YOU'RE THINKING, "I CAN'T SHAKE THIS BAD FEELING."

When you're feeling tense, this visualization may help melt away your fears.

Sit on the floor or lie down and close your eyes. Imagine that you've stepped out of your body and are looking at yourself while you meditate. Observe yourself from afar. Walk a full circle around your body. Now pick up a paintbrush and dip it onto a palette. Starting with your favorite color, brush each part of your body slowly from your head to your toes. Take time to re-dip your paintbrush and choose a different color for each body part. Imagine the stress melting away with each brush stroke and your muscles transforming from tensed to relaxed as the paint touches your skin. Once you've painted your entire body, take a few more deep breaths. When you're ready, open your eyes.

Some studies have found that consistent visualizing can help you reach your potential when combined with practicing. For example, if you're trying to master a particular dance move, imagine yourself executing the move for a few minutes before you physically practice. Don't rush — the visualization should take about the same amount of time as the act would in real life.

"COURAGE IS RESISTANCE TO FEAR, MASTERY OF FEAR — NOT ABSENCE OF FEAR." – MARK TWAIN

Strike a (Yoga) Pose

It's important to find time for yourself – even if it's only for a few minutes in the middle of a busy day. Yoga is about calming your mind and body. Not only can it help bust stress, but it can also relieve pressure in tense muscles.

When trying a new pose, focus on your breathing as you move. Don't hold your breath. You can do these poses as a series, one after another, or you can just try one pose when you want to relax. Hold each pose for 30 seconds to one minute.

YOU WILL NEED:

a yoga mat
a comfortable outfit

Downward-Facing Dog

Sanskrit name: Adho Mukha Svanasana

Get into a plank position with your hands directly underneath your shoulders and your feet hip-width apart. Breathe out as you slowly press your hips toward the ceiling to form an inverted V. Keep equal pressure on your hands and feet.

Why this pose is good for you: Downward-Facing Dog deeply stretches your back muscles and your calves. It's also a good strengthening exercise for your arms.

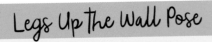

Legs Up the Wall Pose

Sanskrit name: Viparita Karani

Place your yoga mat perpendicular to a wall. Sit facing the wall with your legs straight in front of you. Place a yoga bolster or small pillow several inches away from the wall. Scoot toward the wall, slowly bringing your legs up onto the wall, until your lower back rests on the pillow. Lean your head and back onto the ground. Keep legs straight and locked together and your arms out to your sides in a goal post position, with palms facing up. Take five to ten deep breaths in this position.

Why this pose is good for you: This inversion pose can relieve tension in your back and soothe tired legs and feet.

Cobra Pose

Sanskrit name: Bhujangasana

Lie facedown on the yoga mat. Place the tops of your feet flat on the floor. Bend your arms, keeping your elbows close to your body and your hands palms-down at your sides as if you were about to do a push-up. Spread your fingers wide, then slowly arch your back as you lift your torso upward. Your head can face forward or you can tilt your chin up toward the ceiling. Hold the stretch for five breaths.

Why this pose is good for you: Cobra Pose is a great stretch for your spine and can help reduce lower back pain.

Corpse Pose

Sanskrit name: Savasana

Lie on your back with your legs straight in front of you
and your arms at your sides. Face your palms up and let
your knees drop open comfortably. Take deep breaths as
you rest in this position.

Why this pose is good for you:
Corpse Pose is used at the end of
a yoga routine as a relaxing but
rejuvenating finish.

"IT DOES NOT MATTER HOW SLOWLY YOU GO AS
LONG AS YOU DO NOT STOP." – CONFUCIUS

Clean Your Room

Organization can give you a sense of control. A clean bedroom can instantly make you feel less stressed. You'll waste less time looking for the things you need and spend less time putting away the things you don't need right now. Here's how you can get there.

TO GET ORGANIZED, YOU HAVE TO GET A LITTLE *DISORGANIZED* FIRST. MAKE SURE YOU HAVE ENOUGH TIME TO COMPLETE THIS PROJECT BEFORE YOU START. IF YOU PAUSE IN THE MIDDLE, YOU COULD GET MORE STRESSED!

How to do it:

1. Tackle one space at a time. It might be a drawer, a dresser, or a bookshelf. Remove all items from the space and place them on the floor or a table so you can see everything clearly. Things might get messier before they get clean – and that's OK. You'll also need to clear a space nearby temporarily so you can more easily accomplish step two.

2. Create three piles – throw it away, give it away, or keep it. Now sort your belongings into the piles. Make quick decisions and don't second-guess yourself. If you have problems making decisions, create a "maybe" pile to revisit at the end.

3. When you've finished sorting, put the throw away and give away piles to the side, and start arranging the items you'll keep. Everything should have a specific place that makes sense and is easily accessible. Create a dedicated "staging area" (such as a chair or side table) where you can keep your books, bag, and keys, as well as tomorrow's outfit. A dedicated "command center" (such as a desk or shelf) is a great place to store homework, a planner and calendar, upcoming projects, and school supplies. In other words, your mittens shouldn't be in a desk drawer, and your calculator shouldn't be in your closet.

Here are some more organization tips:

ARRANGE BOOKS BY SIZE, COLOR, OR SUBJECT.

ORGANIZE CLOTHING BY COLOR, SEASON, STYLE, OR OCCASION.

JEWELRY AND ACCESSORIES CAN BE STACKED, HUNG, OR STORED.

ADD LABELS TO FOLDERS, BOXES, OR JARS TO MAKE EVERYTHING EASIER TO FIND.

Set aside 10 minutes to de-clutter every night. It's amazing how much more organized you can feel in just a few minutes!

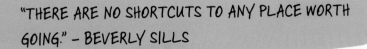

"THERE ARE NO SHORTCUTS TO ANY PLACE WORTH GOING." – BEVERLY SILLS

Simplify Your Wardrobe

One way to de-stress your life is to simplify your wardrobe. Look at all the stuff in your closet or dresser. Do you use all of it? Do you love all of it? Do you need all of it? Do you even want all of it?

The goal of this exercise is to get rid of anything that doesn't fit well, that doesn't make you feel beautiful and confident, and that doesn't feel like "you." If you spend one afternoon purging, there's a good chance you'll end up with a giant bag of donations. Once you've cleared out the clutter, you'll feel lighter and happier. It will be much easier to choose an outfit when you love all of your clothes. Plus, you'll feel great in anything you put on.

DONATE UNWANTED CLOTHING TO AN ORGANIZATION SUCH AS GOODWILL, SALVATION ARMY, OR ST. VINCENT DE PAUL. FORMAL WEAR AND DRESSES CAN BE DONATED TO A PLACE CALLED HOME'S CINDERELLA & PRINCE CHARMING PROJECT.

Create a Capsule Wardrobe

A capsule wardrobe is a minimalist, tightly edited wardrobe that can easily be mixed and matched to create many looks. Did you know that with just 12 items you can create over a hundred outfits? It's true. 4 shirts + 3 bottoms + 4 jackets or sweaters + 1 dress + 3 pairs of shoes = 100 different outfit combinations!

You might not be able to edit your wardrobe down that much, especially if you live in a place that gets really cold in the winter and really hot in the summer. But finding 12 perfect pieces is a great goal for each season's weekly wardrobe.

Many capsule wardrobes are made up of simple styles and basic colors that never go out of fashion, such as a black v-neck T-shirt, a great fitting pair of jeans, and a comfortable pair of sandals. Here are some steps to get you started:

REMOVE ALL OF YOUR CLOTHING FROM YOUR CLOSET AND YOUR DRAWERS.

GET RID OF ANYTHING YOU HAVEN'T WORN IN THE PAST YEAR AND ANYTHING THAT'S STAINED OR TORN.

NOW PURGE ANYTHING THAT'S OUT OF STYLE OR THAT DOESN'T MATCH ANYTHING ELSE YOU OWN.

TRY ON THE REST. GET RID OF ANYTHING THAT DOESN'T FIT WELL OR THAT DOESN'T MAKE YOU FEEL GREAT.

ASSESS WHAT IS LEFT. IF YOU NEED TO EDIT MORE, KEEP CLOTHES THAT ARE IN THE SAME COLOR FAMILY, THAT ARE ESPECIALLY COMFORTABLE, AND THAT CAN EASILY BE MIXED AND MATCHED.

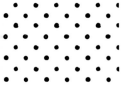

"YOU CAN'T START THE NEXT CHAPTER IF YOU KEEP READING THE LAST." – UNKNOWN

Head Outdoors

Feeling connected to nature is good for you. It can help you feel healthier and happier by bettering your mood, reducing anxiety, and improving brain function. Imagine what a few hours outdoors can do for your soul. When it comes to beating stress, this is as natural as it gets!

Sunlight and fresh air are natural mood lifters. Being outside can help you feel more energized, less stressed, and can increase happiness.

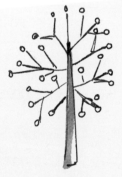

Mindfulness Tip: When you're outside, take time to notice things that really call to you. Maybe it's the color of a flower, the smell of freshly cut grass, or even an ant crawling on a the sidewalk. Savor those things that you're drawn to!

Go outside! Try:

- GOING ON A LONG BIKE RIDE AROUND A NATURE RESERVE OR A LAKE.
- RENTING A KAYAK OR CANOE WITH A FRIEND.
- TAKING A TRIP TO A SKI HILL WHERE YOU CAN PRACTICE YOUR SNOWBOARDING SKILLS.
- GOING ON A HIKE THAT LEADS TO A WATERFALL OR A LOOKOUT POINT.
- VISITING A BOTANICAL GARDEN OR ARBORETUM.
- CAMPING WITH YOUR FAMILY.
- GOING FOR A WALK IN A NEARBY PARK AND TAKING PHOTOS OF TREES OR BIRDS.
- SPENDING AN AFTERNOON AT A PETTING ZOO OR FARM.
- GOING APPLE PICKING WITH FRIENDS.
- TAKING A WALK WITH YOUR FAMILY AROUND YOUR NEIGHBORHOOD AFTER DINNER.
- MAKING A SNOWMAN WITH YOUR SIBLINGS OR SOME FRIENDS.
- OFFERING TO MOW THE LAWN OR RAKE LEAVES FOR YOUR PARENTS OR A NEIGHBOR.
- PLANTING FLOWERS IN A GARDEN OR IN A POT. IF YOU DON'T HAVE ROOM FOR A GARDEN AT YOUR HOME, YOU CAN ALWAYS VOLUNTEER FOR YOUR CITY'S PARKS AND RECREATION DEPARTMENT.
- READING A BOOK ON THE BEACH OR ON A PARK BENCH.

Even if you can't get outdoors right away, there are other things you can do to help you feel more connected to nature. Here are a few ideas:

- CHANGE THE BACKGROUND ON YOUR COMPUTER OR PHONE TO YOUR FAVORITE NATURE PHOTO. SIMPLY LOOKING AT PICTURES OF NATURE CAN HELP YOU DE-STRESS.
- WATCH A DOCUMENTARY ABOUT A NATIONAL PARK YOU'D LIKE TO VISIT.
- CREATE A PINTEREST BOARD OF YOUR FAVORITE NATURE PHOTOS.
- SET UP A WORKSPACE NEAR A WINDOW. NOW YOU CAN DO HOMEWORK WITH A VIEW!
- DECORATE YOUR ROOM WITH PICTURES OF YOUR FAVORITE OUTDOOR SCENES.

"EVERYTHING HAS BEAUTY, BUT NOT EVERYONE SEES IT." – CONFUCIUS

Body Scan

Mindfulness is about being in the present moment with an attitude of curiosity and without judgment. The more you stay in the present moment, the more you'll let go of stressing about things that may happen in the future or things you might regret about the past. This is why a lot of research has shown that people who practice mindfulness are less depressed, less anxious, and less stressed!

The body scan is a mindfulness practice that you can do anytime you have 20 minutes or so. It's important to take your time doing it, spending several minutes on each body part, so that you can really notice physical sensations.

· You begin by lying down on your back, gently resting your arms by your sides about six inches away from your body. You are allowing your legs to simply rest on the floor, noticing your whole body lying here resting.

· Now, turning your attention to your breath, you are seeing if you can simply notice your breath moving gently in and out of your body. You are noticing your belly rising and falling with each in-breath and each out-breath.

· Taking your time, you are shifting your attention from the belly down through to the soles of your feet. You are noticing any sensations you might be feeling. Maybe warmth or coolness? Tingling or tickling?

· After several minutes of noticing sensations, you are shifting your attention to the rest of your feet. You are noticing what sensations are in your toes or heels — maybe pleasure, maybe pain, or maybe nothing at all. Whatever you are feeling, it is perfectly OK. You're just noticing what's there, not trying to create any feelings that aren't there. If you notice any discomfort, see if you can explore the experience with curiosity. You are asking yourself, "What is this sensation I'm feeling? What's it like?"

· As you inhale, you are moving your attention from the feet up into the ankles, first on one foot and the next. You are noticing any sensations that might be in your ankles. Then you are slowly moving to your calves, noticing sensations on the skin of your calves, perhaps feeling the texture of your clothing. Is it smooth? Rough? Scratchy? You are simply observing any sensations that are there, letting them be just as they are.

· When you notice your mind has wandered, as it will, simply return to the sensations in your body. Don't worry about it, or judge yourself for it. This is what our minds do naturally.

· After a minute or two, you are shifting attention to your knees. You are noticing sensations that are at the front of your knees, and the sides, and the area behind your knees. You are taking your time, spending several minutes here. You are just observing with curiosity.

· Now you are shifting your attention to your thighs. What's here? Are your muscles relaxed? What does the sensation of clothing feel like? What does the feeling of contact with the floor or bed feel like beneath your thighs? Is there pressure there? Perhaps discomfort? Or do you notice a softness and warmth? You are remembering that there's no right or wrong way to feel.

· You are shifting your awareness now to your belly. You are focusing on your breathing and the feeling of your belly expanding and contracting with each breath, gently moving, almost like a boat rocking on the sea.

· After a few minutes, you are shifting your attention to your chest. You are noticing your chest rising and falling — a gentle movement with each breath. Perhaps you are even hearing your heart beating. You are taking a few minutes here to simply notice sensations.

· You are shifting your attention now down both arms to the tips of your fingers on both hands, noticing anything that you're feeling there. What are you feeling on the tips of your fingers? Any sensations at all? Moving now to the palms of your hands, what do you notice here? Maybe warmth? Coolness? A sense of moisture or dryness? Perhaps a pulsing? You are spending a few minutes here, just noticing.

·   Now you are moving to the tops of your hands. What's the temperature here like? Is it different than on the palms of your hands? Are there any different sensations here?

·   Moving up through your wrists and forearms, you are noticing any feelings along your lower arms and upper arms. You are allowing the sensations to be just as they are. You are seeing if there's any tightness in your shoulders or upper back – this is a place people often keep their tension.

·   Now, moving to your neck and throat, what sensations are you noticing on your neck? This is another place where many people hold tension and stress. Do you notice any tightness here or feelings of discomfort?

·   After a few minutes, you are slowly shifting attention to your head and face, checking in with the muscles in your forehead and cheeks. Are these muscles relaxed or tight? Do you notice any sensations in your eye sockets or other areas around your eyes?

·   Now you are letting go of sensations in your head and face, bringing your attention back to your breath. You are noticing your belly expanding and contracting slowly with each breath.

·   Taking your time and only when you feel ready, you are gently opening your eyes, stretching your body, turning to your right, and sitting up.

Notice how you feel after doing this body scan. Do you feel different than you did before?

Take a Bath

Baths can be both relaxing and healing. They can soothe muscles, calm some skin inflammations, and help you fall asleep. Taking a bath can even help you feel better when you're sick. When it comes down to it, baths are the ultimate "me" time! So, if you're going to take a soak, you might as well make it extra special. Try one of these bath-boosting ingredients for an easy pick-me-up or calm-me-down.

Mindfulness Tip: As you immerse your body in the water, notice how the water feels against your skin. Is it warm? Silky? Smooth?

HERBAL TEA

Tea is good for your mind and body — so good that you can literally bathe in it! It is believed by health experts that many herbs have healing properties, from relieving pain (chamomile) to calming your nerves (lavender) to healing your skin (mint). Create your own blend that's perfect for your needs right now.

How to use it: Add loose-leaf tea of your choice to a mesh bag with a drawstring top (found at craft stores). Let it soak for the duration of your bath.

EPSOM SALT

Epsom salt is a special kind of salt that can relax sore muscles and tired feet. Athletes often soak in Epsom salt-filled baths to relieve injuries and soreness. It can be found in the beauty or health aisles of grocery stores. Adding aluminum-free baking soda to your Epsom salt bath can make your skin extra soft.

How to use it: While the bathtub is filling, add one cup (250 g) of Epsom salt and two cups (442 g) of baking soda to the water. Soak for about 15 minutes.

BATH OIL

Love essential oils? Bath oils are a great way to add your favorite fragrance to a long soak. Lavender is an obvious choice for a just-before-bed bath thanks to its calming aroma.

How to use it: Make your own bath oil by mixing five drops of lavender essential oil with 1 tablespoon (15 mL) of olive oil in a small glass bowl. Stir well. Pour carefully into the water while the bathtub is filling.

Be careful! Oils can make bathtub surfaces slippery. A non-slip bath mat may help. Wipe the bathtub with a dry towel after use.

OATMEAL

Oatmeal can soothe dry, irritated, or itchy skin. That's why it's used so frequently in lotions for sensitive skin. If sensitive skin or allergies are a problem for you, an oatmeal soak might be exactly what your body needs to calm down.

How to use it: In a blender or coffee grinder, grind 1 cup (155 g) of rolled or old-fashioned oats into a very fine powder. Or buy colloidal oatmeal, which has already been ground. (Don't use instant oats.) Add while the bathtub is filling.

BATH SALTS

Bath salts combine the healing benefits of salt and essential oil for a great one-two punch. You can also try blending two different kinds of salt (such as Epsom and sea salt) or two different essential oils (such as lemon and rosemary).

How to use it: Mix five drops essential oil of your choice with ½ cup (135 g) coarse sea salt in a small glass bowl. Stir well. Pour carefully into the water while the bathtub is filling.

MILK

Milk isn't just for drinking! It's hydrating, soothing, and may improve your skin health. A milk bath will make the water — and your skin — feel smooth and silky. But don't grab a gallon out of your refrigerator — powdered milk is best for baths.

How to use it: While the bathtub is filling, add 1 cup (106 g) of whole powdered milk (found at grocery stores).

"TO FIND YOURSELF, THINK FOR YOURSELF." – SOCRATES

Start a Gratitude Journal

Scientists agree: expressing gratitude is a good thing. Studies have found that it improves your physical and mental health. It also may help you think more positively, since you'll begin focusing on all the good things and the great people that are a part of your life. Even when you're feeling overwhelmed, incorporating gratitude into your daily habits is time well spent.

To begin, set aside at least five minutes before you go to bed each night to reflect on your day and write down something for which you feel grateful. Your entry can be as simple as expressing gratitude for a positive interaction with a friend. Or you can go into more detail and share the many reasons you feel particularly grateful for that friend.

EVERY DAY

All you need is a dedicated notebook. Keep it by your bed so you remember to write in it each night.

When you're feeling down, flip through some old entries. You'll find it hard not to smile.

Here are some tips for making your gratitude journal great:

- TO GET STARTED, THINK ABOUT THE BEST PART OF YOUR DAY OR WEEK.

- FOCUS ON PEOPLE, NOT THINGS. WRITE ABOUT THE POSITIVE INTERACTIONS YOU HAD WITH FRIENDS AND FAMILY — EVEN THE LITTLEST OF MOMENTS MATTER.

- WRITE DOWN WHAT HAPPENED AND WHY YOU ARE GRATEFUL. IMAGINE WHAT LIFE WOULD BE LIKE *WITHOUT* THAT MOMENT OR THAT PERSON. THAT MIGHT HELP YOU DESCRIBE HOW GRATEFUL YOU ARE.

- IF YOU WRITE ABOUT YOUR OWN ACHIEVEMENT, ELABORATE ON HOW YOU GREW AS YOU WORKED TOWARD THIS GOAL. DON'T FOCUS ONLY ON THE GOAL ITSELF.

- IF YOU'VE HAD A CHALLENGING DAY OR WEEK, FOCUS ON WHAT YOU LEARNED FROM THESE CHALLENGES.

- SOME ENTRIES MAY BE MORE ELABORATE THAN OTHERS. MAYBE AN AFTERNOON SNACK WAS THE THING YOU WERE MOST THANKFUL FOR TODAY. THAT'S ALL RIGHT!

- YOU DON'T HAVE TO STICK WITH JUST WRITING — YOU CAN DOODLE OR TREAT YOUR JOURNAL SUCH AS A SCRAPBOOK, ATTACHING PHOTOS, TICKET STUBS, AND MORE.

"ENJOY THE LITTLE THINGS IN LIFE BECAUSE ONE DAY YOU'LL LOOK BACK AND REALIZE THEY WERE THE BIG THINGS." – KURT VONNEGUT

Treat Yourself

Sometimes you need a treat — and this single-serve cupcake recipe will do just the trick. It's a party for one. The reason? Because you said so!

Cupcake for One

YOU WILL NEED:

3 tbsp (24 g) flour
1 tbsp (12.5 g) sugar
¼ tsp (1 g) baking powder
1 tbsp (15 mL) oil
1 tbsp (15 mL) milk
¼ tsp (1.25 mL) vanilla extract

Directions:

Preheat oven to 350 degrees Fahrenheit (180 degrees Celsius). Mix ingredients together in a small bowl. Pour into a cupcake liner in a muffin tin. Bake for 15-18 minutes. Let cupcake cool.

YOU WILL NEED:

1 tbsp (14 g) butter (at room temperature)
¼ tsp (1.25 mL) vanilla extract
2 tbsp (15.5 g) powdered sugar
sprinkles

Frosting
Directions:

Mix ingredients together in a small bowl. (Mash butter with a fork if it's too firm.) Once your cupcake has cooled to room temperature, use a butter knife to spread a thin layer of frosting onto the cupcake. Top with sprinkles.

"WE MUST BE OUR OWN BEFORE WE CAN BE ANOTHER'S."
– RALPH WALDO EMERSON

Be Prepared

Planning is a strategy for managing — and reducing — stress. In fact, planning ahead has the ability to prevent stress before it even starts!

Being prepared is closely tied to being productive. And when you're prepared and productive, you'll have more free time and less stress, which means you'll be happier. Not bad, huh? Here are some simple ways to plan ahead to make tomorrow — and future tomorrows — go more smoothly.

- PICK OUT TOMORROW'S OUTFIT TONIGHT.

- BEFORE YOU LEAVE SCHOOL FRIDAY, LOOK AT NEXT WEEK'S SCHEDULE AND MENTALLY PREPARE.

- CREATE A STUDY SCHEDULE FOR AN UPCOMING TEST.

- PACK YOUR LUNCH AND A SNACK THE NIGHT BEFORE.

- EVERY MORNING, WRITE DOWN THE THREE MOST IMPORTANT THINGS YOU HAVE TO DO THAT DAY.

- SCHEDULE AND STICK TO A BEDTIME. (SEE PAGE 40 FOR TIPS.) DON'T JUST SET AN ALARM FOR WAKING UP, SET ONE FOR BEDTIME TOO.

- CREATE A WEEKLY AND A DAILY TO-DO LIST.

- START SAVING A SMALL AMOUNT OF MONEY NOW FOR SOMETHING IN THE FUTURE.

- ESTIMATE HOW MUCH TIME YOUR HOMEWORK WILL TAKE EACH NIGHT.

- WHEN PACKING FOR A TRIP, PUT TOGETHER COMPLETE OUTFITS INSTEAD OF RANDOM ITEMS.

- ON SUNDAY NIGHT, MAKE A CHECKLIST FOR THE WHOLE WEEK.

- SCHEDULE TIME EACH DAY TO RELAX, DO YOGA, OR MEDITATE.

- BREAK DOWN A BIG PROJECT INTO SMALLER TASKS AND PLUG THEM INTO YOUR SCHEDULE.

- IF YOU KNOW YOU WON'T HAVE TIME TO GET EVERYTHING DONE, ASK FOR HELP IN ADVANCE.

- DO YOUR LAUNDRY EVERY WEEKEND SO ALL YOUR FAVORITE OUTFITS ARE READY FOR THE WEEK.

- PACK YOUR SCHOOL BAG THE NIGHT BEFORE.

- PLAN A "BUFFER DAY" BETWEEN DUE DATES SO THAT YOU COMPLETE ASSIGNMENTS OR PROJECTS ONE DAY EARLIER THAN NEEDED.

- ORGANIZE YOUR TO-DO LIST BY WHAT'S MOST IMPORTANT.

"BE SO GOOD THEY CAN'T IGNORE YOU." – STEVE MARTIN

Be Productive

"Gamifying" is a mental trick. It turns a task into a game by using motivators such as competition, rewards, or time limits. The more you "win," the more you'll want to keep winning . . . and the more productive you'll become. These tricks will help you finish something that you've been avoiding — from an English paper to violin practice to cleaning your room.

Here's one way to stay motivated: if you don't complete the task, you have to delete your favorite apps from your phone. You can always add them back!

SPRINT!

Set a timer for 30 minutes — and work the entire time. Push distractions to the side. When the buzzer rings, take a five- or ten-minute break. Then get back at it! Breaking your task into a more manageable workload can keep you motivated throughout the process.

SET RULES

Get strict with yourself. Make your desk a phone-free zone. Disable the Wi-Fi on your computer when you're working on an English paper. Set a "no social media after 8:00 p.m." rule. Whatever it takes to keep you focused! If you break a rule, take away something for a night such as your favorite TV show or app.

CHUNK

"Chunking" is all about grouping similar tasks together, which makes it easier to focus. When you're more focused, you're more efficient. Can you group all of your reading and note-taking into one night this week? Can you finish writing those two papers in one session? Can you complete all of this week's chores in one afternoon?

MAKE A BET

An accountability partner is someone who checks in on your progress and holds you to your goals. You could partner up with someone for the whole school year and offer each other a little friendly competition. Or simply tell a parent "I'm going to finish this geometry assignment by 8:00 p.m." Getting another person involved might be the kick in the butt you need.

DANGLE A CARROT

Promise yourself a treat if you complete a certain task or goal. For example, if I get my homework done before 8:00 p.m., I can watch my favorite TV show. Or, if I get my paper done, I can turn my phone back on.

DON'T BREAK THE CHAIN

Keep track of your productivity on a chart. On a horizontal axis, write the days of the week. On the vertical axis, write this week's daily goals. For example, complete my homework by 9:00 p.m., stop using social media after 8:00 p.m., get 9 hours of sleep, work on my presentation for 30 minutes, etc. When you meet a goal, shade in that box for that day.

MASTER THE TO-DO LIST

A to-do list is motivating because it feels great when you get to cross something off. But if your to-do list is too long, you'll never get that satisfaction! Instead, try creating more than one list — such as a daily and a weekly version. The weekly list keeps you organized while the daily list can help you focus on three things to complete each day. Or try making two to-do lists for the week — one for your personal life and one for school. The visual separation will help you feel less overwhelmed. If you're feeling burned out as you chip away at your school list, move to the personal list — or vice versa. Make it fun by giving yourself a point for each item you complete.

UNDERSTAND YOUR HABITS

Being productive means getting tasks done quickly and efficiently. In order to do this, you'll have to pay attention to your habits. Track your progress for one week and keep notes. How long did it take to do you homework every night? Why do you keep getting distracted? Why did it take so long for you to start? When do you feel most creative and energized?

Get Some Sleep

It's easy to let your sleep suffer when you have a lot going on. But when you get a good night's rest, you'll wake up feeling energized and ready to take on the day.

Sleeping DOs

1. EXERCISE

Work out each day, and you'll be more likely to fall asleep at night. Exercising earlier in the day is better. Breaking a sweat late at night can keep you up for hours.

2. CHAMOMILE TEA

Chamomile tea is caffeine free and is said to help induce sleep. A warm glass of milk can do the trick also. Just don't drink too many liquids before bed. One glass provides all the soothing you need.

3. BREATHING

You should be able to fall asleep within 15 minutes of lying in bed. Breathing can help make that happen. Try the Equal Breathing or Relaxing Breath exercises from page 7 to help send you to dreamland.

4. SCHEDULE

Your bedtime and wake-up call should be the same time every day, even on the weekends. Sticking to a schedule helps train your internal clock. Before you know it, you'll be hopping out of bed one minute before your alarm goes off.

5. HIDE THE CLOCK

If you can't fall asleep, the worst thing you can do is stare at the clock. It will only stress you out more and make it even harder to fall asleep. Stop that vicious cycle before it starts and don't keep a clock by your bed. If you use your phone as an alarm, turn it upside down and keep it out of reach.

Sleeping DON'Ts

1. TV

Many people like falling asleep with the TV on or watching their favorite show right before bed. But the light and noise aren't good for those who are trying to catch some ZZZs. Even if you fall asleep quickly, it will take you longer to reach the quality sleep zone, or REM stage, which means you'll wake up drowsy.

2. PHONE

Is your phone the last thing you check each night and the first thing you check each morning? That's not good! While it's fun to browse social media feeds in bed, phones emit blue light, which messes up your internal body clock.

3. NAPS

Long naps can alter your sleep patterns. If you really need an afternoon snooze, keep it to a 20-minute catnap.

4. CAFFEINE

Caffeine is a stimulant that begins to slowly wear down within a few hours, but it can stay in your body for eight hours or more. That means you should avoid caffeine after lunch or it could disrupt your sleeping patterns at night.

5. HOMEWORK IN BED

Don't bring your homework or your laptop to bed. Save it for the desk or dining room table. Otherwise you'll find yourself stressed out in bed, which definitely won't help you fall asleep.

"DREAMING, AFTER ALL, IS A FORM OF PLANNING." – GLORIA STEINEM

The 60-Minute Wind-Down

1 HOUR BEFORE BEDTIME . . .

Take five minutes to wrap up any conversations, homework, or TV shows. Now turn off all screens. The light from bright screens signals to the brain to stop producing melatonin, a hormone which helps promote sleep. But falling asleep is exactly what you're trying to do!

55 MINUTES BEFORE BEDTIME . . .

Pick out your clothes for tomorrow, make your lunch, or pack your bag. Simple routines like this — when they are repeated every night — can send signals to your brain that it's almost time to sleep.

40 MINUTES BEFORE BEDTIME . . .

At night, our body temperature drops a bit. Take a warm bath for 15 minutes. When you get out of the tub, your body will cool down quickly and send a signal to your brain that it's time for bed. For an extra treat, add the bath salts from page 31.

25 MINUTES BEFORE BEDTIME . . .

Dim the lights. The easiest way to regulate your sleep cycle is through light. If you don't have a dimmer, think about switching out the light bulbs in your lamps with ones that have a softer glow (look for lower wattage and less lumens).

24 MINUTES BEFORE BEDTIME . . .

Stretch lightly for a few minutes. Try the Legs Up the Wall Pose (page 17). End with Corpse Pose (page 19).

20 MINUTES BEFORE BEDTIME . . .

Hop into bed. Make sure you're comfortable and cozy. Put on a pair of socks if your feet are too cold. Pick up your favorite book or write in your journal for the next 15 minutes.

5 MINUTES BEFORE BEDTIME . . .

Put away your book or journal and shut off the lights completely. Try the Relaxing Breath from page 7, which naturally helps you fall asleep quickly.

BEDTIME . . . ZZZ . . .

The majority of teens don't get enough sleep. Without a good night's rest, you may have trouble concentrating, learning, listening, and more. Sleeping in on the weekends isn't the answer. There's no such thing as "catching up." If you want to wake up feeling energized, you need to prioritize sleep and stick to a schedule, which means getting up and going to bed the same time every day.

Do You Need Help?

If you've ever thought about harming yourself or others, seek help right away. Turn to page 47 for a list of resources.

The exercises and ideas in this book offer help for short-term stress.

They are not cures or treatments for more serious, long-term issues, such as

chronic depression, suicidal thoughts, self-harming behavior, disordered eating,

addiction, post-traumatic stress disorder, and generalized anxiety disorder.

Symptoms of more serious mental health issues, such as depression or anxiety, can include any or all of the following:

- LETHARGY AND/OR FATIGUE
- RESTLESSNESS
- FEELINGS OF GUILT
- TROUBLE SLEEPING INCLUDING OVERSLEEPING, INSOMNIA, AND RESTLESS SLEEP
- LACK OF STRENGTH OR ENERGY
- LACK OF INTEREST IN DAILY ACTIVITIES AND HOBBIES
- CHANGES IN APPETITE
- WEIGHT GAIN OR WEIGHT LOSS
- DIFFICULTY CONCENTRATING, MAKING DECISIONS, AND REMEMBERING
- LACK OF SELF-CONFIDENCE
- PERSISTENT FEELING OF SADNESS
- FEELING AS THOUGH YOUR LIFE ISN'T WORTH LIVING
- PERSISTENT PHYSICAL SYMPTOMS IN RESPONSE TO YOUR EMOTIONS (SUCH AS GETTING A HEADACHE OR STOMACHACHE AS A RESULT OF SADNESS OR ANXIETY)
- THOUGHTS OF DEATH OR SUICIDE
- MOOD SWINGS
- SOCIAL ISOLATION OR PERSISTENT FEELINGS OF LONELINESS
- CHANGE IN ENERGY LEVEL
- CHANGE IN SELF-ESTEEM
- FEELING EASILY OR OVERLY IRRITABLE
- FEELINGS OF HOPELESSNESS AND PESSIMISM
- APATHY
- EXCESSIVE CRYING
- SIGNIFICANT CHANGES IN DAILY BEHAVIOR
- LACK OF MOTIVATION
- FEELING "EMPTY"
- SLOWNESS OF ACTIVITY
- RACING THOUGHTS AND/OR EXCESSIVE WORRY
- FEELING A SENSE OF IMPENDING DANGER
- EXCESSIVE SWEATING, TREMBLING, OR SHORTNESS OF BREATH

If any of these negative feelings have been affecting you regularly for two weeks or more, you may need some extra attention. It's important to seek help as soon as possible, especially if your symptoms are affecting your relationships, your health and well-being, or your ability to fulfill your responsibilities.

How to Ask for Help

If you or a friend needs help, there are many people and resources you can turn to. A doctor, social worker, or school counselor can offer professional help. If you need help figuring out how to contact one of these people, reach out to a trusted friend, family member, or teacher.

On a day-to-day basis, friends and family members can keep you on track. Don't forget that asking for help makes you stronger, not weaker.

In addition to seeking out professional help, you can ask supportive, reliable, confident friends and family members to . . .

HELP YOU STAY POSITIVE.

LISTEN WHEN YOU NEED SOMEONE TO TALK TO.

HELP YOU CREATE AND MANAGE A SCHEDULE.

REMIND YOU THAT OTHER PEOPLE STRUGGLE TOO.

MOTIVATE YOU TO FINISH YOUR HOMEWORK ON TIME.

MAKE YOU LAUGH.

HELP YOU GET YOUR CHORES DONE.

PRAISE YOUR PROGRESS.

REMIND YOU THAT YOU WILL FEEL BETTER SOMEDAY.

WAKE YOU UP ON TIME — NO SNOOZE BUTTONS ALLOWED.

GO FOR A WALK WITH YOU.

MAKE DOCTOR APPOINTMENTS FOR YOU.

GIVE YOU PEP TALKS AND TELL YOU WHY YOU'RE GREAT.

WHO CAN HELP

National Suicide Prevention Lifeline
www.sptsusa.org
1-800-273-TALK (8255)

Substance Abuse and Mental Health Services Administration's National Helpline
www.samhsa.gov
1-800-662-HELP (4357)

National Eating Disorders Association
www.nationaleatingdisorders.org
Crisis text line: text "NEDA" to 741741
1-800-931-2237

S.A.F.E. Alternatives
www.selfinjury.com
1-800-DONT-CUT (366-8288)

Gay, Lesbian, Bisexual and Transgender National Hotline
www.glnh.org
1-888-THE-GLNH (843-4564)

The National Center for Grieving Children & Families
www.dougy.org
1-866-775-5683

National Runaway Safeline
www.1800runaway.org
1-800-RUNAWAY (786-2929)

Planned Parenthood
www.plannedparenthood.org/info-for-teens
1-800-230-PLAN (7526)

National Sexual Assault Hotline
www.rainn.org
1-800-656-HOPE (4673)

National Domestic Violence Hotline
www.thehotline.org
1-800-799-SAFE (7233)

National Alliance on Mental Illness
www.nami.org
1-800-950-6264

Read More

Falligant, Erin. *A Smart Girl's Guide, Getting It Together: How to Organize Your Space, Your Stuff, Your Time—and Your Life*. A Smart Girl's Guide. Middleton, Wis.: American Girl Publishing, 2017.

Loewen, Nancy and Paula Skelley. *Lunch Lines, Tryouts, and Making the Grade: Questions and Answers About School*. Girl Talk. North Mankato, Minn.: Capstone, 2015.

Reber, Deborah. *Doable: The Girls' Guide to Accomplishing Just About Anything*. New York: Simon Pulse, 2015.

Internet Sites

Use FactHound to find Internet Sites related to this book.

Visit *www.facthound.com*

Just type in 9781515768210 and go.

Aubre Andrus is an award-winning children's book author with books published by Scholastic, American Girl, and more. She cherishes her time spent as the Lifestyle Editor of *American Girl* magazine where she developed crafts, recipes, and party ideas for girls. When she's not writing, Aubre loves traveling around the world, and some of her favorite places include India, Cambodia, and Japan. She currently lives in Los Angeles with her husband. You can find her website at www.aubreandrus.com.

A mindfulness practitioner for almost 40 years and a lifelong educator, Dr. Karen Bluth is faculty at University of North Carolina at Chapel Hill. Her research focuses on the roles that self-compassion and mindfulness play in promoting well-being in youth. She is author of *The Self-Compassion Workbook for Teens* (New Harbinger Publishers) and co-creator of the curriculum *Making Friends with Yourself: A Mindful Self-Compassion Program for Teens*.